THE ANTI-PREP MANUAL
...OR
"SEE YOU LATER, ALLIGATOR."

Created and written by Tom Shadyac
Art director Perk Hull
Illustrations by Dave Merrill and Mary Bausman
Photography by Charlie Brown
Anti-prep consultant Manny Mencia

Punch Publishing Inc.
a wholly owned subsidiary of:

Punch Posters, Inc.
P.O. Box 2001
Falls Church, Va. 22042
(703) 642-5456

Manufactured in the
United States of America.

Printed by
Hagerstown Bookbinding & Printing Co., Inc.
Hagerstown, Md. 21740

First printing October 1981.

ISBN 0-941714-00-4

"To be preppie, or not to be preppie?
That is the question . . .
I will choose the latter."

Bill Shakespear, 1981.

Acknowledgements

I would like to thank the following people for their contributions to this public service book:

Ron "Happy" Hier, Jerry "The Vacuum" Burkot, Tony "California" Kogak, Dave "The Machine" Black, Pete "Dow" Jones, Tippy and Kathy, D. I. Shadyac, Charlie Brown, and Tina.

Special thanks to Chris for her untiring inspiration, Rick for his expert legal counsel, the boys at Sigma Chi who accepted me without khaki pants, Dave Merrill for his rush jobs, Manny Mencia without whom this book would never have been finished, and Mom and Dad, the world's greatest Anti-Prep parents.

T.S.

Contents

Introduction

It all starts with a simple Izod shirt covering the upper torso. Soon Khaki pants and Topsiders garnish your lower regions. By strange forces, you are compelled to add a button-down shirt, a plaid watch-band, and a navy blue blazer. Your beard is shaved, your hair is cut and your nose is raised. You can no longer deny the self-evident truth — YOU ARE A PREPPIE!

This is the sad description of millions of Americans who were forced by the malignant "incurable" preppie cancer to forfeit their freedom of choice and adopt a stringent, meticulous, stuffy lifestyle. Underneath the plaids, the madras, and the motifs are people who are crying for help; people who want to be freed from the clutches of preppiness.

This Anti-prep Manual is the answer to your desperate cries! We will explore a new discovery in the causes of preppiness, test your level of

10

Izod infection, and then discuss the known cures. Finally, there is a dramatic moving tale of one family's struggle with the elite syndrome.

So tear off your Izod, put on your hardhat, grab a Budweiser, and read on. . . . See you later alligator. . . .

Foreword

You can often recognize a contagious disease by the sound of its name; rabies, scabies, herpes, and preppies . . . YES, PREPPIES — the name given to a disease which impairs mental functions, distorts perception, and dulls taste!

In the past, Preppiness was the most dangerous illness of all because no vaccine existed to curtail its spread. But today we live in an age of miracles. If we can walk on the moon, split the atom, and put up with Iranians, why can't we cure Preppiness? The answer is . . . WE CAN!

Rutherford Byron Snodgrass and
Priscilla Martha Snubnose
before reading the Anti-Prep Manual . . .

Rutherford Byron Snodgrass   Priscilla Martha Snubnose

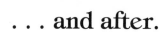

. . . and after.

"Rudy"

"Cilla"

15

Chapter 1

PREPPINESS
AS A
BIRTH DEFECT

The Genetic Cause of the Prep Disease

Until recently, Preppiness was believed to be caused solely by environmental factors: social clubs, monetary worth, private education, country club membership, and the like. However, research at the Anti-Prep Institute has shed new light on a different cause of this ailment. After years of laboratory and bedroom testing, the Institute has published a genetic theory which states that Preppiness can be inherited directly through the genes of the parents.

Before studying Preppies, the Institute had been conducting experiments on pregnant, fashion conscious, New York females or JAPPS (Jewish American Pregnant Princesses). Photographs taken of the fertilization process between the sperm of the Jewish American Prince and the eggs of the Jewish American Princess reveal that all JAP offspring possessed a unique type of chromosome: DESIGNER GENES or KLEINO SASSOONIUS.

This discovery prompted the theory that like Jappiness, Preppiness could be attributed to (or, more properly, blamed upon) the genes of the parents. To test this theory, the Institute collected a cross section of Preps, mated them, and monitored the entire fertilization process.

The Prep subjects were paired into two groups:

EXPERIMENTAL GROUP 1:
Prep Male with Prep Female

EXPERIMENTAL GROUP 2:
Prep Male/Female with Freak (Hippie) Male/Female

A CONTROL GROUP:
(Normal Male with Normal Female) was also monitored.

Test Results

GROUP 1

As expected, members of Experimental Group 1 (Prep mating with Prep) always gave birth to Ultra-Prep offspring. The following photographs, taken through a high-powered microscope, show Preppie sperm combining with Preppette eggs. Notice that the result is always a Preppie zygote (see illustration). Thus, scientists concluded that Preppiness was, in fact, carried in the genes of the parents!

PREPPIE SPERM

PREPPETTE EGG

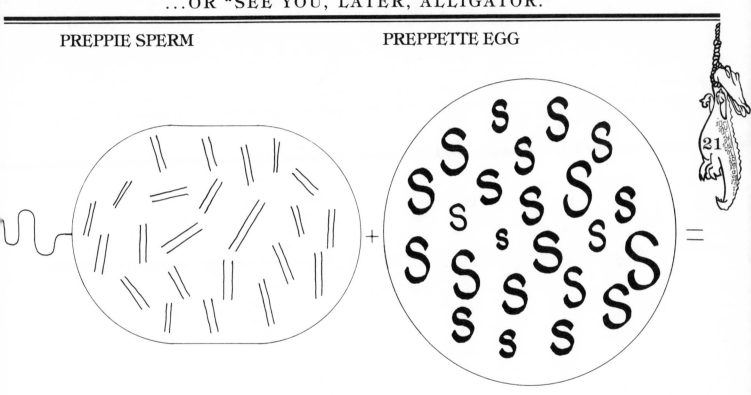

Turn page for result.

RESULT: PREPPIE ZYGOTE

PREPPIE SPERM   PREPPETTE EGG

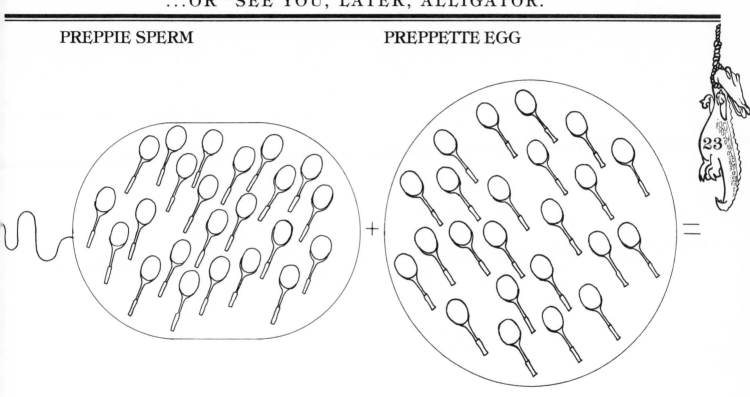

Turn page for result.

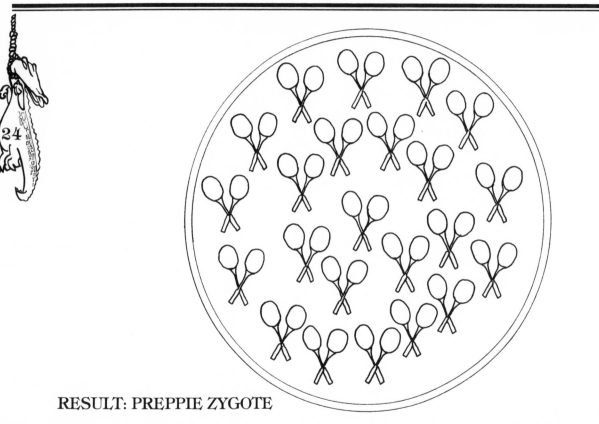

RESULT: PREPPIE ZYGOTE

PREPPIE SPERM   **PREPPETTE EGG**

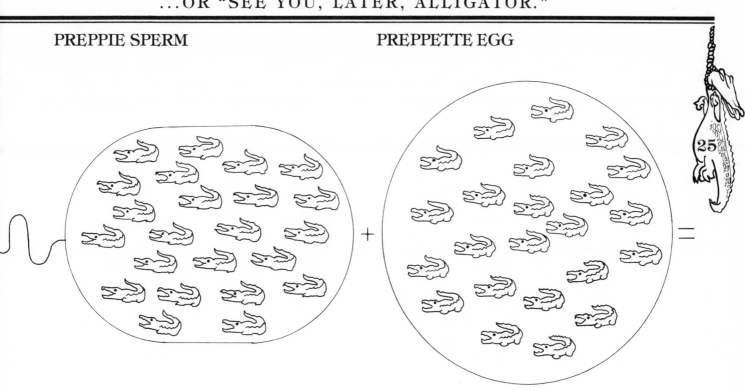

Turn page for result.

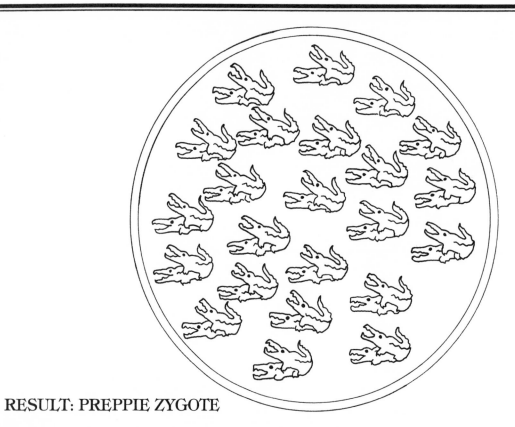

RESULT: PREPPIE ZYGOTE

Having identified these Preppie genes, scientists then took X-rays of the developing fertilized egg. These startling X-rays show that the first behavioral signs of Preppiness can be found in the position of the fetus, itself.

Observe the Preppie fetal position. Notice that the head, nose, and chin are always pointed upward (see illustration).

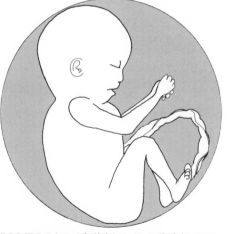

NORMAL FETAL POSITION

PREPPIE FETAL POSITION

CONTROL GROUP

The dramatic results of Group 1 and 2 are a significant contrast to the normal pairings of the Control Group. In every case, normal parents gave birth to normal offspring. These children exhibited no signs of Preppiness and grew up to be normal Americans — they graduated from community colleges, were married, soon divorced, had 2.3 children, and drove wood-paneled station wagons.

29

GROUP 2

The results gathered from Experimental Group 2 (Prep mating with Hippie) supported the Institute's genetic theory. As expected, the children of mixed parents showed a combination of Preppie and Freakish behavioral traits. For example, they attended public school but chose to wear uniforms, shagged to Led Zeppelin, and smoked marijuana only with initialed rolling papers.

Preppie Offspring

The offspring of the Prep parents continued to display Preppiness from the moment they were born. When the doctor administered the traditional slap, the Preppie infant sued. As the illustration demonstrates, Preppie babies insist on monogrammed breast feeding.

The following pictures show the Preppie child's disinterest in normal toys (A) compared to his fascination with Preppie toys (B).

(A) A preppie infant is uninterested in normal toys

(B) . . . but is fascinated by preppie toys

31

Conclusions

Preppiness has proven to be a birth defect, an illness deeply ingrained in the blood of the infected parent's offspring. In other words, Preppie parents will be cursed with Preppie children. But don't be too discouraged. There are precautions that can be taken to prevent the transmission of these infected genes.

Chapter 2

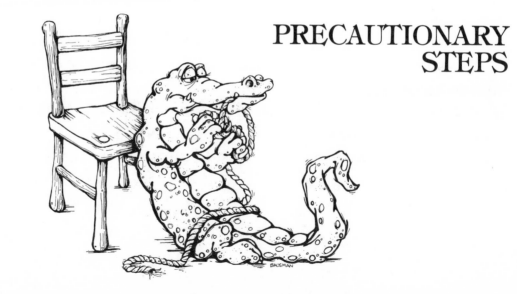

PRECAUTIONARY STEPS

Preventing the Preppie Disease from Spreading.

THE HABIT BREAKS THE HABIT
OR
PRIESTHOOD PREVENTS PARENTHOOD

To assure that you will not have preppie offspring, transform yourself from a "man of the madra" to a "man of the cloth." In other words, you must forfeit your LAY habits. The sisterhood's very name will dictate your mating behavior — NUN of this, NUN of that . . .

Your new religious lifestyle should control your urge at every *conceivable* occasion.

2. TOPSIDERS AS A BIRTH CONTROL DEVICE

If used properly (and at the right moment) topsiders can prevent the birth of Preppies. During the preliminary passionate moments, the Preppette should remove her topsiders, place one firmly between her knees and *SQUEEZE*.

She should maintain this position as long as necessary. (Usually 20 years is sufficient.)

35

3. THE ORAL CONTRACEPTIVE

The oral contraceptive can be used by either partner. It is the easiest birth control devise to use — simply open your mouth and say *NO!* Unfortunately, it is not very effective as the rejected mate often counters with irresistable, preppie inducements: LIQUOR and MONEY.

The three measures just mentioned are effective in preventing the birth of new preppies but do nothing to alleviate the preppiness in the parents. Despite the seeming malignancy of preppiness, there are cures available. But before discussing these cures, it's important to test your level of preppiness so you will know which anti-prep program to select.

38

The Preppie Test

The following test will determine whether your thought processes have been infected by the Preppie germ. Each question has one or two normal answers and one Preppie answer.

Test Questions

1. Which container holds more alcohol?

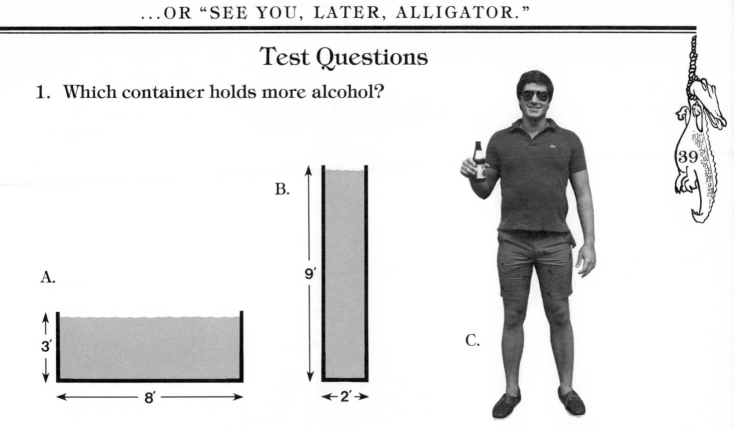

A.

3′

8′

B.

9′

2′

C.

(The Preppie answer is C.)

39

2. What do you see in the ink blot below?

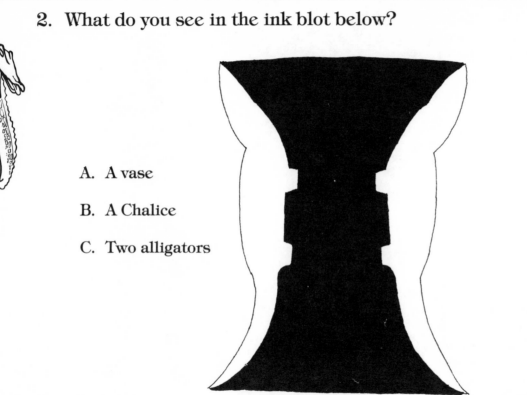

A. A vase

B. A Chalice

C. Two alligators

3. Complete the following sentence with your preference of the choices below: "I would rather _____ ."

   A. Get a summer job.
   B. Die.

(The Preppie answer is B.)

4. Which type of "Fox" hunting do you prefer?

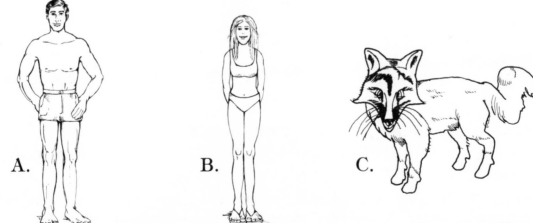

A.   B.   C.

(The Preppie answer is C.)

5. Which is your favorite sex object?

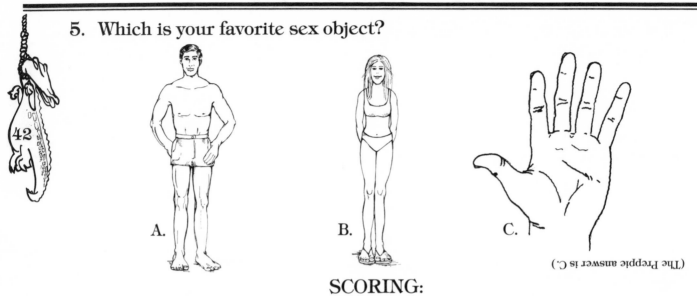

A.   B.   C.

(The Preppie answer is C.)

SCORING:

Give yourself one point for each Preppie answer chosen. A score of **5** is the highest level of Preppiness, while 1 is the lowest and thus, most normal.

If you have selected the Preppie answer in any of the questions, seek immediate help. Cures are offered in the next chapter.

Chapter 3

CURES FOR PREPPINESS

CURE NUMBER ONE:

THE SURE FIRE SOLUTION

Known as the "all or nothing plan," this cure is the most drastic available and, due to its irreversible consequences, is recommended only to those who scored a 5 on the preppie test. When aimed properly, the sure fire solution really gets to the "heart" of the trouble. As one expert put it, "With this cure, you can't miss." Thanks to this immediate and highly effective solution, the alligator is no longer an endangered species.

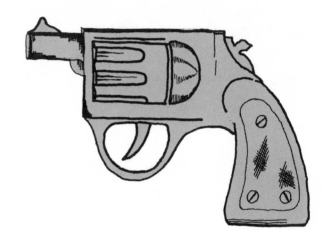

CURE NUMBER TWO:

REINCARNATION

Closely related to cure number one, reincarnation is based on the premise that God would not make the same mistake twice. It is recommended to those who scored a 4 on the preppie test.

On June 17, at 8:00 a.m., a preppie chose cure number one.

On June 17, at 8:01 a.m., this mule was born. There is little chance that it will grow up to be a preppie.

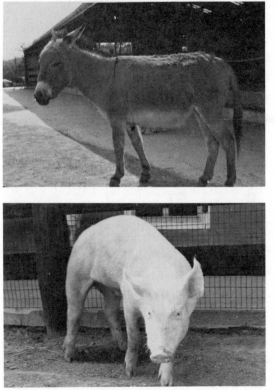

A Reincarnated Preppette

45

CURE NUMBER THREE:

BANKRUPTCY

The quickest way for a Prep to be tossed out of the elite circle is to declare bankruptcy. No prep can remain on the social register without money in the cash register. If one truly wants to break out of the Preppie mold, he must lose all of his inherited dollars.

There is no better way to go from wealthy to worthless than to make bad investments. Therefore, we have provided the Anti-Preppie with the following list of stocks and products, all of which are guaranteed losers:

1. Iranian Travel Agencies Inc.
2. Hebrew International Pork Products
3. Afro-Sheen Tanning Lotions
4. Puzzles For Poland Inc.
5. King Family Birth Control Ltd.

Another efficient way to get rid of your money and cure your Preppiness is to donate it to an unpreppie charity. Here are a few suggestions:

The United Negro Fund
Alcoholics Anonymous

The Save An Alligator, Shoot A Preppie Society

CURE NUMBER FOUR:

47

APPEARANCE

The most fundamental manifestation of the Prep disease is reflected in one's outward appearance. From head to toe, a Prep looks the part. To cure yourself of Preppiness, you must give up traditional mentality. Here are a few suggestions to help you get back on the road to normality:

1. Most Preps have neatly coiffed, closely cropped, blonde hair.

If you fit into this category, change your hairstyle to the Anti-Preppie look.

Tyler Jarvis Washington illustrates the ultimate Anti-Prep hairstyle.

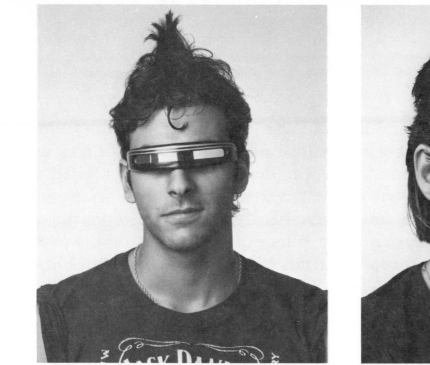

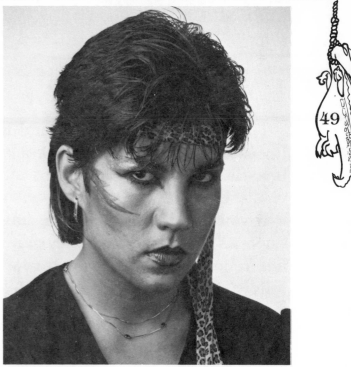

49

Johnathan Byron Sidley is transformed into Johnny Snotty with this punk hairstyle achieved with his finger and an exposed light socket.

Carla Rodriguez demonstrates the most popular Anti-Prep hairstyle for women, The Illegal Alien Look.

CURE NUMBER FIVE:

CLOTHING

The symbol of the traditional Preppie wardrobe is the alligator, alias Lacoste. As we all know, the Prep's love of the alligator borders on beastiality. To rid yourself of the Preppie disease, you must condition yourself to detest the alligator.

If you are a true Prep, you have undoubtedly accumulated dozens of Lacoste shirts whose collective value runs quite high. At first, we do not recommend that you throw them all away. Instead, practice the following Anti-Prep ritual — GATOR-BITING.

50

Gator-Biting

To help you become a true Gator-Hater, the sport of Gator-Biting was devised. In the following pictures, the complete ritual is demonstrated by two reformed Ultra-Preps.

(1) Locating the Gator.

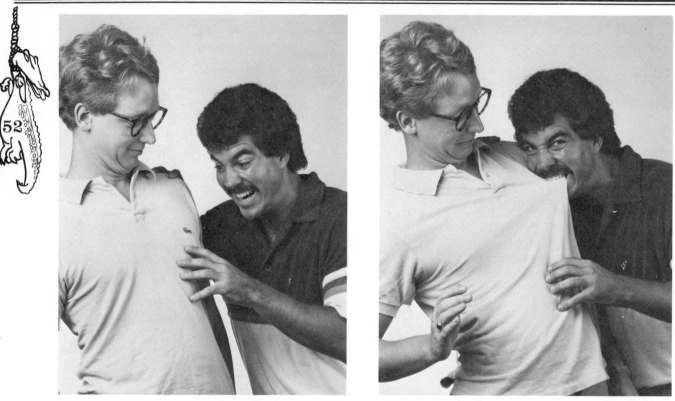

(2) Approaching the Gator.   (3) Biting the Gator.

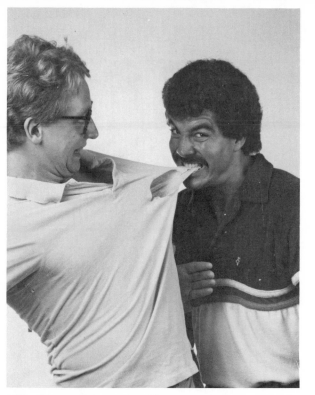

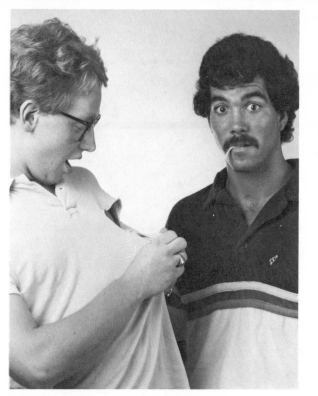

(4) Detaching the Gator.

(5) Detachment Complete.

53

(6) Chewing the Gator.

(7) Swallowing the Gator.

(8) Disposing of the Gator.

Gator-biting will help you end your love affair with the alligator. Practice it on a friend, an enemy (preferably one smaller and weaker than yourself), at parties, or anywhere people meet. Remember, the average Izod is less than 50 calories so bite away!

One note of caution: Be careful when performing the ritual on a female Preppie. You don't want to bite off more than you can chew.

55

While the preceding cures are essential for expelling any tendency toward Preppiness, they do not offer a long-term Anti-Prep program. To fulfill this vital need, an Anti-Prep maintenance routine is offered in the next chapter.

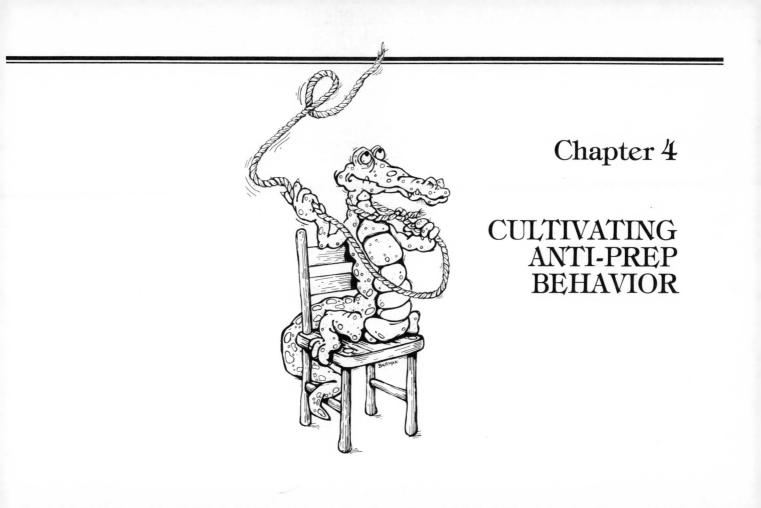

Chapter 4

CULTIVATING
ANTI-PREP
BEHAVIOR

Just as Preppiness is a commitment to a certain style of living, so too is Anti-Preppiness. You will need to make a commitment if you are ever to rid yourself of every last vestige of Preppiness.

Forget about the Platters and the Supremes! Listen to Ted Nugent, the Dead Kennedies, memorize the Woodstock album.

And no more dining at "The Club" with mummy. Instead feed your face at Jack-In-The-Box and Howard Johnson's. Quiche Lorraine and filet mignon are out of the question. Try ordering black-eyed peas, bagels, and burritos. As for washing it all down, who needs Heineken when there's Rolling Rock, Billy Beer, and Pabst?

Preppiness can get you if you don't watch out. Look at yourself in that Mercedes! It's not you, Joe. The Anti-Prep knows there's more room in a Chevy van, better gas mileage in a Chevette, and more excitement in a Pinto.

Don't look to George Bush and Franklin D. Roosevelt as role models when there are so many great Anti-Preps to emulate: Abe Lincoln, Fred Sanford, Cheech and Chong. . . .

The point is, for everything Preppie there's something Anti-Preppie; language, sex, monogramming, dancing . . . yes, even dancing. Use the suggestions that follow to keep yourself free of Preppiness.

Dancing

In order to dance (shag) like a Prep, it is necessary to use your hands and spin your partner. To break yourself of this habit, try dancing with your hands tied firmly behind your back. Use the leather shoe laces from your old topsiders.

Without the hands, the Prep ritual of shagging becomes a frustrating act of futility. After a few weeks of treatment, untie yourself and feel free to dance in public without looking like an idiot.

Drinking

To say that Preps love drinking is the understatement of the 1980's. In fact, doctors report that drinking is the one area in which no known cure for Preppiness exists. Even electro-shock therapy proved useless as treated Preps simply kept drinking until they were too blasted to feel the pain.

As one doctor put it, "You can take the Prep out of the drinker, but you can't take the drinker out of the Prep."

Marriage

To continue their traditions, Preppies must marry within their class and bloodlines. One simple way to destroy this inbreeding is to marry out of your social class and WASPish ethnicity. For the best Anti-Prep results, we suggest marrying an Iranian student.

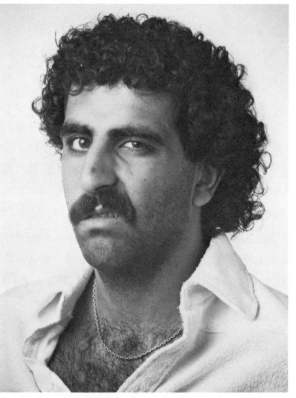

Take Beheshniev home to "Mummy"

Sex

Preppies are adept at social intercourse — as long as it is kept out of the bedroom. Remember, preps make money, not love. Consequently, anyone who has a successful love life is probably not a preppie. But in case you need a pointer or two, we have compiled a list of unpreppie sexual behaviors.

A. FEMALES

1. DO NOT have sex with preppie men. Especially, if you are hoping to establish a long-term relationship. Male preps relate sex with banking — the minute they make a withdrawal, they lose interest.

2. It's o.k. to scream. The rules of etiquette do not apply to the bedroom. There is no reason to act as if you are in the Harvard library. Feel free to make noise — It wards off preppie spirits.

3. NO MIRRORS.

B. MALES

1. DO NOT practice alone. Since Preppies are their own greatest love objects, they have a lot of sex alone. We suggest you try having sex with a partner for a change.

2. During sex, like in everything else they do, Preppie men have to be on top. Anti-Preppies should try the bottom.

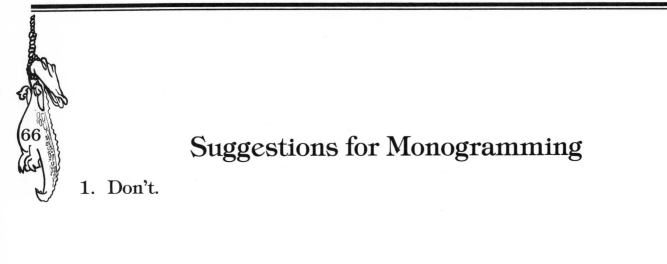

66

Suggestions for Monogramming

1. Don't.

67

Suggested Anti-Prep Phrases

The Preppie disease even permeates daily speech. How often we hear of Preps who "Dine With Mummy" while waiting to "Sail To The Virgins" . . . Prep-talk is an "awesome" problem. To protect yourself from "Blowing Your Doughnuts" over the Preppies' verbal onslaught, rinse your mouth daily with Anti-Prep phrases.

SUGGESTED ANTI-PREP PHRASES

To help take the vanity out of your vocabulary, practice the following Anti-Prep sayings:

1. "Pass the chitlins." (Preppies and soul food go together like Linda Lovelace and braces.)
2. "I'm on the wagon." (For a Prep, every day is an alcoholiday.)
3. "All men are created equal." (Preppies support equality about as much as Playtex supports the braless look.)
4. "Let's buy it at K-Mart. ("Discount store" is a foreign language phrase to a Prep.)

Other phrases to help you guard against Prep-talk are:

"I'm only human!"
"I can't afford it."
"I bought it on sale."
"We need the money."

The following list of words should be removed completely
from your vocabulary and memory:

Trust Fund	Ego	L. L. Bean	Awesome
Mummy	Country Club	Madras	Tortoise Shell
Self-Stimulation	Khaki	Monogram	Private
Tradition	Yacht	Ancestry	Aristocracy
Allowance	Topsider	Initials	Uniform

70

Suggestions for Insulting a Preppie

"Preppies are insulted when you offer them a drink — but they always swallow the insult."

Insulting a preppie is not only easy and fun, but it also serves a vital anti-prep function. Listed below are several suggestions for criticizing an infected friend.

"A preppie male's love life is best summed up by that famous American Revolution group — THE MINUTE MEN."

"You know what makes a preppette look good? — Distance."

"When it comes to having sex, a preppie has to hand it to himself."

"What do you give the preppette who has everything? — Penicillin."

"Take away a preppie's mirror and you've taken away his best friend."

"The proper description of a preppette: a human gimme pig."

"A preppie man could never be convicted of rape — the evidence would never stand up in court."

"The ideal man for a preppette has blue eyes and green money."

"A preppie's idea of sowing wild oats always results in a crop failure."

"Preppettes promise to love, honor and obey until debt do us part."

"When preppies meet, it's an I for an I."

"Preppettes aren't blonde on their mother's side or their father's side, but on peroxide."

71

72

Recognizing Preppie Falsehoods

The Preppie Motto: "If at first you don't succeed, lie, lie, again."
Talking to a preppie is a lot like opening a can of Schlitz Malt Liquor — look out for the bull. Lying is a means to boost one's importance and thus has become an accepted practice amongst preppies. As an anti-prep, it is important to recognize these fibs and to expel them from your conversations. Here are the most frequently voiced preppie lies:

"I was a guest at the Last Supper."

"I'm good in bed."

"I'm a natural blonde."

"I got a ticket for jay walking — on the Atlantic Ocean."

"I'm well endowed."

"Howard Hughes worked for my father."

"I was once in a street fight in Venice."

"I'm not that kind of a girl."

74

Uses For Your Old Preppie Apparel

Since they spent so much of daddy's money on their wardrobes, most preps beginning the anti-prep program are understandably reluctant to simply toss their expensive preppie clothes in the trash. Although the garbage can is the best place for them, there are other anti-prep uses for your traditional "garb." Try the following suggestions with your stockpiled preppie fashions:

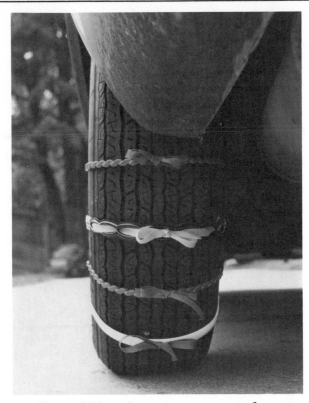

1. Your old hair barrettes are great for extra traction in the snow.

2. Topsiders make an excellent poopoo scoop.

75

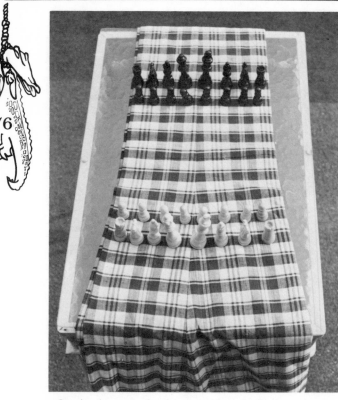

3. And your plaid pants are perfect as a portable chess board.

4. Girls, an old kilt skirt is easily transformed into a pup tent that sleeps 4.

77

5. Or how about using those old kilt pins to keep up with the latest new-wave styles.

6. Topsiders also make a great chew toy for your dog.

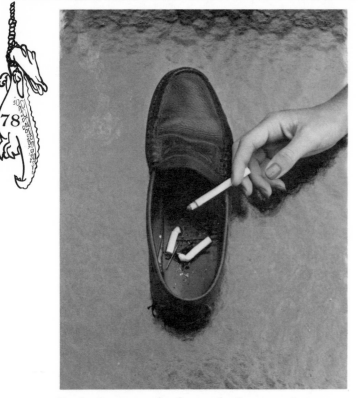

7. And a penny loafer is ideal as an ash tray.

8. Your old yachting cap makes a perfect container for your next specimen.

79

9. And why not keep your old purse handy as a car sick bag?

10. Use your Ray Bands as a disguise for your once preppie Golden Retriever.

Chapters three and four examine some but not all of the ways to deal with the preppie sickness. There are other ways to eliminate the disease; poison darts, letterbombs, and nose surgery, to name just a few. In fact, one family found a unique, but very effective way to expel preppie spirits. Their story is revealed in the next chapter.

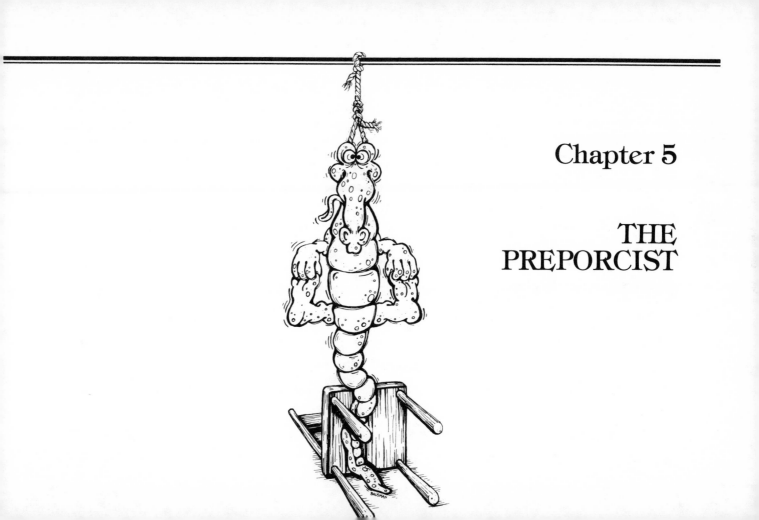

Chapter 5

THE PREPORCIST

82

The Preporcist

Constance and I had long given up our preppie lifestyle when we had Jim, a healthy, 8-pound, baby boy. We wanted him to grow up to be normal, immune from the preppie germ which had dominated our lives. But as he grew, it became more and more obvious that he was a carrier of the prep disease.

Jim had everything a boy needs to turn out to be normal; he had a short middle class name, was educated in public school, and was raised in an ethnic neighborhood. We even made him get a job in the summer. But despite our efforts, Jim (who preferred to be called James) developed into an ultra-prep.

We didn't know what caused the prep infection, but the signs were apparent since his birth. As a baby, he insisted on khaki diapers and would eat only imported baby food. While other children played tag, James played the stock market. He became infatuated with preppie objects: his wallet, his money, and himself. At his first trip to the zoo, he stared for hours at the alligators.

As he got older, his preppiness reached obnoxious levels. He never even had a pimple! Judge for yourself. Here's a copy of a letter we received from him when he ran away to Andover:

> Dear Parent$,
> $chool i$ awe$ome. Gue$$ what I need?
> $ee you $oon.
>
> $incerely,
> Your $on, Jame$ the $econd.

After reading that letter, we knew we had to take immediate, drastic action to free him from snobbery. We called the only person who could help us now — THE PREPORCIST.

83

It's the job of a preporcist to dispel the preppie spirits which control physical and mental functions of a human. We didn't know how he could destroy the preppiness in our son. We didn't care. All we wanted was a normal boy.

Our preporcist, Father Manuel Juan Sanchez (a full-time employee of Jack-In-The-Box) arrived at our house with a gym bag full of anti-prep items. Constance and I led him to James' room, which now reeked of stale beer. Under the instructions of Father Sanchez, we took the alligator shirt off our sleeping son and clothed him with a Fox t-shirt from J.C. Penney. Once the garment touched his skin, he woke up in a frenzy and we were forced to tie him to the bed. Because of this strong reaction to the anti-prep stimuli, we had to leave on James' hideous patchwork pants.

With James clothed in the Fox shirt and outrageous trousers and helplessly bound to the bed, Father Sanchez began the dangerous ritual. He hung pictures of Fred Sanford around the room, placed jewelry from Woolco on James' neck, and sprinkled Boone's Farm Wine over him. James' face contorted with pain as the peasant products touched his body. He squirmed frantically as the Father blessed himself with the sign of the dollar and began reading anti-prep materials. Mercilessly, he read aloud the Emancipation Proclamation, and the By-laws of the NAACP. It was too much for James to take; he spit up khaki vomit which soaked Sanchez. But the preporcism continued as Father read on. He began chanting over and over the ultimate anti-prep incantation: "K-Mart is your saving store, where your dollar buys you more. K-Mart is your . . ."

James turned bluer than his Andover blazer. We watched in horror as the head of the Fox on James' shirt turned completely around. With this incredible occurrence, James' body went limp. James showed no signs of life.

As Constance began to cry uncontrollably, James woke up and curiously looked himself over. "James" I shouted excitedly. Then James spoke the words that I will never forget; "My name's Jim, Dad. And what the hell am I doing in these butt-ugly pants?"

Thank God, Father Sanchez, and K-Mart — our son was cured.

87

Epilogue

So you see, Preppiness is curable. Using the cures and suggestions offered in this manual for the public's well-being, you *can* rid yourself of the dreaded disease. The author sincerely hopes that this book has been helpful. The rest is up to you. Be brave, be daring, be courageous, and above all . . . BE NORMAL!